TEN
SIGNS OF A
LEADERSHIP
CRASH

Also by Stephen Mansfield

The Character and Greatness of Winston Churchill:
Hero in Time of Crisis

Then Darkness Fled:
The Liberating Wisdom of Booker T. Washington

Forgotten Founding Father:
The Heroic Legacy of George Whitefield

The Faith of George W. Bush

The Faith of the American Soldier

Benedict XVI: His Life and Mission

The Faith of Barack Obama

The Search for God and Guinness

Lincoln's Battle With God

Killing Jesus

Mansfield's Book of Manly Men

The Miracle of the Kurds

TEN
SIGNS OF A
LEADERSHIP
CRASH

STEPHEN
MANSFIELD

BLACKWATCH
DIGITAL

Author photograph: Isaac Darnall

Published in Nashville, Tennessee by Blackwatch Digital

ISBN: 978-0-9977647-3-4 (print)
ISBN: 978-0-9977647-4-1 (ebook)

TABLE OF CONTENTS

Foreword

by Dave Ramsey
Radio Host and Bestselling Author

Even though it happened two decades ago, it feels like only yesterday.

I was sitting in my recreation room, looking into the eyes of the young pastor across from me. Yet those eyes let me know that he wasn't grasping what I was saying. His vacant stare told me that he was hearing my *words*, but not my *heart*.

That was frustrating—and painful.

You see, this young man was an *incredible* communicator. Over the years, I've been blessed to share the stage with some world-class speakers, both in the mainstream and in the Christian world. This young man didn't take a backseat to any of them. He had a God-given gift for explaining an idea so people could understand it. He could take a story, mix in just the right amount of humor, and lift listeners to new heights. What's more, his natural talents were refined through hours of hard work.

Like I said, he was world class.

If I mentioned his name today, you wouldn't recognize it. There was a time, though, when he had the potential to become his generation's Billy Graham. I told him as much, but I also told him that he needed to make some changes. He had mastered his craft, but he had never mastered his character.

And that was a problem.

"*If* and *only if* you deal with these leadership and personal behavior blind spots will you be the person and leader I can see you becoming," I said.

He didn't hear me. For whatever reason, he *couldn't* hear me.

So, the damage continued to escalate. Eventually, after a string of lost positions, two broken marriages, a bankrupt church, and countless other embarrassments, he simply wandered off into obscurity. Now, he's just a cautionary tale.

Thankfully, I've had the chance to count many great leaders in the business world and in ministry as dear friends. Those relationships have been a true blessing to my life. Yet too many times, my joy has been offset by watching one of them hit the wall and blow up. In the blink of an eye, all they were—and all they could have been—has burned to the ground.

Unfortunately, whenever a leader crumbles, it's never just a personal or individual problem. Many more lives end up being devastated by the leadership failure. We have all seen the carnage. In some cases, we've been *part* of the carnage. The story of this young, talented pastor serves as just one illustration of what you and I have seen so many times.

Looking back, I realize that I was trying to convince him to address several of the points made in the book you're holding right now. That's because my friend, Stephen Mansfield, has had his own front row seat for far too many crashes. He's also worked hard to keep other leaders from skidding off the tracks. That passion and experience make him uniquely qualified to address this topic honestly and intelligently.

When I first read this material, my heart started cheering. It's encouraging to remember that crashes don't *have* to happen. We just need to watch for the signs in our own leadership lives and the leadership lives of those close to us.

Practical, clear teaching—like what Stephen provides in this book—is the only way to ensure that those of us in leadership maximize our potential and avoid landing on the junk heap of broken lives and careers. The ten signs he identifies aren't easy or comfortable to think about, but they are personal, clear, and correct. What's more, you can use them to spark great discussions with your own leadership team as you strive to hold each other accountable.

Stephen has given you a tremendous gift that you'll thank him for over and over again. This book is going to make a difference, and it's going to make a difference for leaders the world over.

Introduction

_____

WHY DO LEADERS CRASH?

I'm not asking why they fail. The answer to that question has to do with how they lead, what gifts they have, and whether they were ever in the right position to begin with.

No, I'm asking why leaders crash.

Why does the congressman blow up a promising political career with an affair? Why does the CEO lose a position that could have netted him millions of dollars by mishandling a hundred thousand dollars? Why does the NBA star with an adoring, beautiful wife have a clumsy sexual episode with the room-service girl? Why is the respected governor of a state found in the mountains of a foreign country hiding from the fallout over news he's been having an affair? Why does the revered NFL quarterback forever damage his reputation by texting photos of his private parts to a woman who doesn't want to see them? And a thousand more. Why?

A large portion of my life's work has centered upon the answers to these questions. This started during my twenty-year career as a pastor. Several of the leaders on my staff at that time had major moral collapses and, along with the rest of my wonderful team, I helped these leaders rebuild. Then we restored them to their roles. Word spread that we did this pretty well. Other churches, and soon other types of organizations, called to ask for our help. Before long I found myself consulting with private firms, churches, the families of the famous, and even the staffs of congressmen and senators.

What each of these wanted was someone who could fix the damage. They wanted to recover after the pastor misbehaved or the CEO resigned over what he did to the intern or the NFL coach blew it with alcohol or the rock star flipped out.

I liked helping them all. I should say, too, that we were very successful. Aside from what expertise we might have in this field, it helped that people called us because they were in desperate circumstances. They were hurting and eager for help. This meant they cooperated with us. They invested. They healed. Better days came for them. It was gratifying, and we are still seeing huge success in this unusual work.

However, a day came when I realized something very valuable. I realized it because of what I had heard over and over again during the hours of discussion I conducted about crashed leaders. In nearly every case, I heard the same statements from those who surrounded the fallen—from wives and husbands and children and best friends and associates.

All of them told me after the crash that there were signs of what was coming they hadn't been able to see before the crash. "I see it so clearly now," they would say. "How could I have missed it? I wish I had said something." They would sometimes stand in my office in clusters and agree that they had all seen the same signs of trouble, but none of them had known what to do.

they see the problems in hindsight but not until the damage was done.

I knew exactly what they meant. For years, I had been taking notes on what those around a crashed leader would point out as the "signposts" on the road to the crash. It was fascinating. I don't mean this callously. It was fascinating because in almost every case, people around a leader who crashed saw important signs very early on and simply did not act. What is important for the moment is not that they didn't act. It is the fact that they saw trouble coming, even if they didn't know what to do when they saw it. The point is there were signs. People saw them. Things might have turned out differently.

I began to compile what people had told me and what I had seen for myself about the signs that signaled a crash. I compared notes with consultants who handle these types of high-visibility crashes. We all saw that while we might have been using different language, we had become aware of the same signs of a personal decline.

I realized that while I will always help fix crashes—it is important work, particularly in our time when moral failures among leaders do so much damage—I could help even more by teaching what

I had learned about the signs of an oncoming crash. I started calling this "Lessons from the Leadership Crash Postmortem."

In other words, if I could show people what to watch for in their friends, family, and associates that warned of a crash, I could do far more good than by repairing institutions and lives after the explosion. I could give corporate cultures and leadership teams of every kind—even husbands and wives—language to use for what they saw but couldn't describe. I knew this could help stave off expensive, humiliating, life-ruining crashes.

This is exactly what I'm doing in this little book. I am going to describe the *Ten Signs of a Leadership Crash*. I'm going to list the *lessons of the leadership crash postmortem*. I'm going to explain the ten very common behaviors that are almost always evident in the downward journey of a leader. Perhaps not all of these are involved in every crash story, but most of them are, and knowing just a few of them could save millions of dollars, years of humiliation, hundreds and sometimes thousands of jobs, and much lost good that might have been done.

What if someone had stopped Bernie Madoff? What if a friend knew what to watch for in Tiger Woods? What if someone had courageously confronted Bill Clinton before that first time? What if friends and family had known what to watch for in Bill Cosby's life, or Lance Armstrong's, or Richard Nixon's, or Jim Bakker's, or Brett Favre's, or the pastor of that 3,000-member church in Detroit, or the CEO of Stanford Financial? What might Penn State have been spared by some courage and ethics once the signs appeared?

We can always fix things after the crash. My team and I are good at this. So are many others. Far better is to recognize the signs of a looming crash and intervene. This can save billions of dollars from lost production, the costs of repair and, even more, what is often lost to human lives.

The stakes are high. The need is great. Let's get to it.

1. Being Out of Season

THE FIRST AND PERHAPS MOST IMPOR-
tant sign of a leadership crash is not usually something people notice about a leader. It's usually
something a leader notices about himself. It is often
missed because it's hard to define and almost mystical, but it is one of the most important indicators in
a leader's life. It is simply this: being "out of season."

Sounds simple, doesn't it? I can't adequately
describe how important this is or how often it
comes up. It looks something like this: The CEO is
not where he really ought to be. He knew there was
a time a while back when a change was supposed to
happen. He and his wife had agreed he would move
back to his hometown and open a one-man shop.
It was a done deal. Then things got busy. He didn't
make the move when the moment was right.

Now, he's out of season. He feels it every day. He's overstayed his welcome, gone beyond some kind of invisible boundary for his life. He isn't as good at what he does now. He doesn't enjoy it as much. There is a growing strain in relationships. Walking in the door doesn't feel as normal as it once did. It's like driving a car with the tires out of alignment. There's more bump. More noise. More fuel required. Less enjoyment. And the vibrations are shaking all kinds of things loose.

It is just true. Our lives are measured in some way. There are seasons to life, and I mean more than seasons of high school or college or middle age or retirement. I mean seasons within the big seasons we all recognize.

This is a sign of the leadership crash that most fascinates me because it is more art than hard science. In fact, I believe that discerning it is one of the great arts of life and leadership.

That actress leaves the hit series she is privileged to be cast in long before she should. She had a "golden gig." But she got ambitious. She left the hit show for bigger things. We haven't seen her since. The famous athlete can't seem to retire at the top of his game. He has to try for another record. Or another ten million. Or another standing ovation. He becomes an object of admiration. Then pity. Then scorn. Then he leaves the field one day nearly in dishonor. If he had left three years earlier, he would have been a legend with his name intact and a reputation he could bank on for the rest of his life.

I had the privilege of spending many hours with entrepreneur and CEO Richard Scrushy around the time he went through the horrible events that eventually put him in jail for half a decade. He told me he could remember exactly when things started going badly for him. It was about the time he knew he was supposed to resign from HealthSouth, the stunningly successful healthcare company he founded. But he didn't do it. He will tell you that every painful thing that has happened to him since started because he was out of season. He once said this to me: "At a critical moment in my life, I missed a season change—and it nearly destroyed me."

Not everything that is important to our lives is scientifically verifiable. Not everything critical is measured with a gauge and reported in a number. My wife being happy is essential to my life—and so much else. But detecting what makes her happy is a matter of feel, of paying attention, of sensing, perhaps of keeping a journal, and certainly of being aware that my wife's happiness is something I am responsible for, something that shapes my whole world. But it is invisible, emotional, murky, maddeningly ethereal, and often elusive. Yet, trust me—when I get it right, joy of every kind graces my life. Get it wrong? Misery for us all.

Most of the important things in life are like this: invisible, mystical, and immeasurable. It's the same with being in season. You can't measure it with a GPS. It isn't marked out on a calendar. You know it because you are paying attention to it. You know it because you are watching carefully. You know it because you've been in season before. It was wonderful. You've also been out of season before. It sucked. So, you scan your life in search of the one and to avoid the other.

Your spouse can help you. Your friends can too. Your clergyman can if he or she knows you well enough. Your personal covenants—what you promised yourself, your spouse, your children, God, and maybe your band of friends—can serve as guides. Most of this knowing when you are in season and when you are not, though, is about feel. It's about realizing that there are invisible seasons that define our lives—not just biological seasons or relational seasons—and that part of the art of happiness and greatness is to identify your seasons and conduct yourself accordingly.

Here is what I want you to know: Every man or woman I've ever worked with who made a mess out of their lives told me that they "weren't supposed to be there." They were supposed to get out of that dating relationship, out of that partnership, home from that overseas assignment, off of that field, out from under that boss, free from that culture, back to that safe place or the role that was truly a fit.

Don't get out of season. Don't overstay your welcome. Don't blow past that inner sense that the current arrangement is at an end. Don't ignore the invisible seasons of your life and leadership. It leaves you vulnerable, set up for trouble, out of sync with every important person in your life, and apart from the best version of you. Be in season.

2. Choosing Isolation

IN EVERY SINGLE CASE THAT I'VE EVER consulted in, the leader being out of season was part of the matrix of trouble. Second to it in importance—and in the number of times it has been mentioned to me—is some form of isolation.

Everyone who is engaging and likable enough to lead well has a gang, a posse, a band of brothers around them. Some are lifetime friends, some are new acquaintances, and some are kindred spirits. The wise leader realizes that these people are there for a reason. They are fun, of course, but they are also familiar with each other. They know what makes for good and bad days, know the look in the eye that means a fight happened at home or that something wonderful happened or that someone is about to get punched.

The wise man empowers his band of brothers. He relies on them for their radar about his life. He realizes that these people can be an early warning system, that if they are allowed to speak freely their affection and insight will make them valuable guardians of his soul. He sticks close to them, asks them to always speak the truth to him—just as he will do for them. He builds a culture around himself of honesty, loving confrontation, and permission to intervene.

Now, I am referring to a devoted band of brothers or sisters here. What you don't want is just fans. May you have fans, but if you only have fans in your life they will get you killed. They think everything you do is amazing, and they would not dare speak up to correct or warn you. They just want to worship you. Remember this: Your fans can get you killed.

We also don't want to be surrounded by sycophants—those people who are so dependent on us for income, ego fulfillment, or meaning in life that they would never open their mouths about anything difficult for fear of losing what we provide. These people, sweet as they may be, should be loved but not relied upon for feedback about the important issues in our lives.

Then there are the "uninvested buddies." They are merely looking for a good time. If you get drunk and destroy your life, it's all a bigger laugh for them. If your marriage falls apart because the waitress was hot that night, they have a hotter sister to introduce you to. They aren't invested. They didn't sign up to make you better. They signed up for the party.

It's your devoted friends, that band of brothers, whom you want to stick close to. You want to insist they talk to you about anything they see in your life. You want to enlist them in helping you grow just as you are willing to invest in their ascent in life. This is true friendship, and this is what you need to be a great spouse, a great parent, a great leader, and a great soul.

So, what's the danger sign to look for? It's when a man pulls away from his band of brothers and isolates himself. When a leader does this it is almost the same thing as that leader wearing a T-shirt that says, "I'm pushing you away so I have room to screw up my life." His band of brothers may not know exactly what to do about this isolation, but they feel it. They also feel the danger of it.

Leaders usually isolate themselves for three reasons. The first is their view of authority. The arena of religion is where we see this played out most often. Perhaps you've watched a situation where a local pastor suddenly decides he's an apostle, or a bishop, or the Lord of Lords. His view of his spiritual authority elevates him in his own mind and in the minds of his sycophants into an almost unreachable state: "I'm an apostle and you're not. I hear the voice of God, and you don't. I can interpret the Scriptures properly, and you can't." Usually, that sound you hear two years later is the sound of this man crashing. His sense of authority pushed away anyone who might have spoken helpful truth to him.

This doesn't just happen in the church. It can happen in corporate culture, government, the military, even in a two-man accounting firm. If a leader comes to believe that he is in some way unapproachable because of his title, his gifts, or some other form of superiority, he's giving in to pride, and that pride is positioning him for a crash. No one who knows him well is near enough to warn him about the dangers of the fifth gin and tonic or the well-built girl at the gym who's making a play for him even though he's married or the questionable accounting methods he's begun using. A crash is coming. Remember: *Isolation insulates from information, inviting infamy.* There's a saying you can live with!

A second reason for isolation is hurt. Human beings are like most animals: when wounded, they curl around their wound to protect it. They don't want the wound touched, reopened, or exposed to further damage. With human beings, there is also a pride factor. *I'm hurt. I'm weak. I don't want you to see me like this.*

More than half of the cases I've worked with have involved leaders who were hurt, who isolated themselves to nurse their wounds, and who thus left themselves open to the forces that created their crash. I can tell you these stories by the hour. I'll tell you only one now.

A CEO I know got hurt because her husband flirted with a sweet young thing at a party. She moved to their lake house to nurse her hurt and to punish her husband. Her friends knew something was wrong. They even found out where she was, but they didn't pursue, didn't understand that her isolation was a warning sign. The company then asked a handsome young college intern to take some mail and a second laptop to the CEO's remote, romantic, red wine-filled lake house—you know, the one with the sexy hot tub and amazing view, all isolated so you can go *au naturale*. The CEO ended up sleeping with the muscular young intern. Why? Hurt. Isolation. Weakened resolve. No band of sisters to say, "Oh, no you don't. You'll have to go through me if you intend to mess up your life." And a family, a leader, a company, and a young man were damaged—in some cases terminally.

Solitude is healthy in small doses, particularly if it's about recharging and having space to breathe.

Isolation is unhealthy in any dose. It's about pushing away the healthy. It's often about bitterness and revenge. It's a killer.

Finally, there is guilt. When we do what we know to be wrong, we isolate so we aren't found out. We isolate because we see those we are deceiving through a different lens. Things aren't normal. They can't be. The former ease can't be there when we are stealing or getting high or keeping a lover on the side or descending into the porn pit or conspiring in some destructive way. We feel guilt. We don't want to feel it with those who know us and might notice the telltale signs. We pull away.

Never has the crash of a leader I've been asked to fix not involved a season of intentional isolation that everyone recognized later—when it was too late.

Here's the deal: Isolation is a distress flare. Fight it in your own soul. Be courageous to confront anything that tries to drive you into your own remote emotional jungle. And love your friends enough to pursue them. I can't tell you how much damage has been done because friends sat around wondering what to do when a lifetime friend pulled away.

Let me close this with a story that captures everything I have to say about pursuing friends and those we love. There is a wonderful African-American church that has a wonderful men's ministry and all because there is a wonderful men's ministry leader named Taylor. This devoted man led that phenomenal group of loving, passionate, adventurous, largely African-American men for years. Then something hurtful happened, the kind of thing that occurs in churches when senior pastors change and vision changes with them. So Taylor got hurt. Deeply. And he resigned and left.

He was embarrassed. He didn't know how to process it all. He felt best in isolation. He locked himself up in his house, wouldn't answer the phone, wouldn't see anybody, and thought he could get through it—just Taylor and God. He was actually in decline.

Well, the hundreds of men in that wonderful men's ministry at that wonderful church were disturbed. Thankfully, Taylor had taught them to love each other well. They had no intention of letting Taylor go quiet and wounded into the bitter night. So, they got his wife's permission and they went camping—in Taylor's yard. They literally pitched tents, brought in food, and sat around with big signs Taylor couldn't help but see from his windows: "Taylor, We Love You," "Talk to Us, Taylor," "We Aren't Leaving Without You," "Taylor, You're an Idiot. Get Out Here."

Did Taylor come out of his house? No. He called the police. He was angry. So the police show up. Taylor's wife and a few members of the Church Occupation Force tell the police what's going on. When the two policemen have heard everything, one of them says, "I wish the folks at my church cared about each other this much. You stay right here until this fool realizes how many people love him." And the police start patrolling the makeshift camp to make sure all is well—for the campers!

Then the police decide to help. Every day they stop by Taylor's house, wade through the campers, eat some of the amazing barbeque that the guys are cooking in hopes of "smoking Taylor out," and knock on Taylor's door. Every single day: "Sir, we've been asked to make sure you're okay. We've received calls. Sir, are there any guns in here. Sir, are you alright? Are you in any danger of harming yourself?"

Of course, none of this overzealous policing is necessary but it is legal and it does make a point. More importantly, it brings Taylor to the door once a day and this gives the men camping in his yard a chance to shout their love.

Finally, Taylor breaks. There are tears, apologies, group hugs and—because it's a men's ministry—massive amounts of food. All is restored. Why? Because a group of men pursued. They didn't let isolation become the norm. They didn't sit around scratching themselves and saying, "Whatever happened to ol' Taylor? He was a good guy. Haven't seen him in years." No, they decided that Taylor and the friendship and the good they all did together was worth taking a week off and risking everything to win Taylor back.

Pursue those who are in trouble. Pursue because isolation kills. Thus endeth the lesson.

3. Defining Episodes of Bitterness

WE ALL SUSTAIN WOUNDS IN OUR LIVES. Most of them heal up and are forgotten. Some, though, continue to bleed. We think about them again and again. Bitterness springs from them. All our lives we ponder how some folks wronged us and how it might feel to get back at them. We fantasize about how wonderful it would be if somebody came to apologize.

These big, remembered-all-our-lives wounds—the ones that stoke a powerful sense of bitterness—are so important that I've started calling them "Defining Episodes of Bitterness." Untended, they can be killers.

When Richard Nixon was a young man, he sustained a great many emotional wounds. He was embarrassed by his father's low station in life. He was treated roughly for being a Quaker. He seldom got the girl. In fact, he once offered to drive one couple around on their date because he was secretly in love with the girl but he hadn't won her heart. The other guy did. Imagine that humiliation: driving the girl you love around town on a date with another guy. Such humiliations compounded in Richard Nixon's life. All his public life the press picked at him and haunted everything he tried to do. Even when Nixon was vice president of the United States, President Eisenhower famously mistreated him, which deepened the humiliation and the pain.

By the time Nixon got to the White House, he was a bitter man with a big smile. It led to his downfall. He hated and he wanted revenge. He illegally spied on people, even people from his old high school. He didn't want to politically defeat his enemies; he wanted to carpet-bomb their lives. He had to win. No matter what.

This led to a break-in at a Washington, DC, apartment complex called Watergate, to a cover-up, to the matrix of lies and deceptions he and his men used to conceal their deeds, and ultimately to the resignation of the president of the United States.

Here is the point. During the worst days of Watergate, Nixon would often fly into a rage or fall to his knees in tears, pound the floor, and scream about what "they" had done to him. Who were "they"? Those kids back in high school. More than one aid said that sometimes Nixon, in his grief and bitterness, could hardly distinguish between the wounds of the moment and the wounds of fifty years before. It had all rolled into one.

The soul has a memory like an elephant. Either we forgive offenses or they will cycle in us through the years, gaining strength and recruiting still other offenses. Bitterness is the snarling, vengeful feeling that lives in us as a result. It's poison. It permeates all we do. It can destroy us.

When we are bitter, we feel justified in treating other people harshly. When we are bitter, we feel entitled to any pleasure or privilege. When we are bitter, we rehearse the wrongs done to us and press their imprint deeper into our souls. When we are bitter, we drive the very people we need away.

David Gergen, a Nixon administration official, wrote in his book *Eyewitness to Power*, "We all fight bitterness...Richard Nixon allowed bitterness to deform his soul." This is the danger. Bitterness can take over. It can deform. It can distance us from the strong beings we were meant to be.

I cannot offer this warning too strongly. The biggest disasters I've tended came about because a small offense from a leader's past eventually triggered a bigger offense, a bigger rage, and ever more destructive behavior. So, as in one case, the gifted general drifts into an alcoholic haze mumbling about what they did to him at the academy years ago and how it has somehow become his wife's fault. Then, more alcohol, and he hits her. Repeatedly. And his career is over. Why? Because hazing went too far forty-five years ago at West Point and the general is a great warrior but a small soul and can't let it go.

He loses. His wife loses. His children and grandchildren lose. The US army loses. The nation loses.

Remember what I've said: The soul has a memory like an elephant. It's wrapped in Velcro. It holds on to whatever we let stick to it. We only become healthy when we take time to peel off whatever offenses threaten to work like cancer in our souls.

Watch for bitterness in yourself. Watch for it in others. Confront it boldly. Get the help you need. Otherwise, it sneaks in through the door of other wounds and takes control. And your genius, like the genius of Richard Nixon, is lost in the toxic bog of bitterness.

Let go of bitterness

4. Evading Confrontation

IT WAS AGONIZING TO WATCH THAT child abuse scandal unfold at beloved old Penn State. You remember. Jerry Sandusky, former Penn State assistant football coach, was accused of abusing dozens of boys during sports camps right there on the campus. It turned out that another coach had seen him and had reported it when it all first happened. In fact, he had reported it to legendary coach Joe Paterno. Papa Joe, in turn, told several people and eventually word got to the president of Penn State, so we are told.

And that's where it stopped. Because Sandusky was planning to leave his coaching position not long after his sexual misdeeds were first reported, no one did anything. And, if what investigators reported was true, Sandusky went on to abuse dozens of other children in the years that followed.

Now Penn State is devastated. A decade and a half of heroic deeds on the gridiron were expunged from the record books. A dozen school officials have been fired. Many experts believe that Penn State will never recover. And the revered Papa Joe Paterno is dead. His last months were the worst of his life.

It was all horrible. I have friends who played football for Penn State who wept on my shoulder over what happened to their dear school and its team. A friend on the faculty told me that school health officials were dealing with waves of depression among the students because of the scandal.

But this is what I will never forget. It was when Jerry Sandusky, the man who caused this destruction, flatly stated in an interview, "No one ever confronted me about child abuse."

That's it. Word for word. And when I first heard him say it, I thought he was a liar and said so out loud. Now investigators have come to the same conclusion. Listen: No one—ever—confronted—Jerry Sandusky—about sexually molesting—a child!

My God!

Why? They were cowards? They didn't know what to do? They weren't sure of procedure? No one thought it was their place? Everyone assumed someone else would do it?

I don't know. Frankly, I don't care. Horrors happened while those who knew about them refused to take the battle to Sandusky's door.

My God!

Please hear what I am about to say: There is no healthy person, family, or organization of any kind without well-intended confrontation. It is essential. Without it, chaos and our lesser natures rule the day.

Most people hate confrontation. They fear what others will think or they fear confronting someone and then being hated for it. So, they wring their hands and hope anyone else will step up to challenge the man who is drinking too much or the

Confrontation cannot be avoided

woman who was seen coming out of another man's hotel room or the guy who took cash from the till.

Of course, it gets even more mundane than this. Few people are courageous enough to tell the boss he's being inappropriate with his jokes or to tell that friend his grammar is keeping him from a promotion or to tell the father that his son has a terrible reputation. It's all too time-consuming, too risky. We convince ourselves it's not our business.

Too bad. It *is* our business. You got a "confrontation permit" when you decided to live among human beings, when you decide to lead, or when you let yourself care about another human being. You have no choice. You have to confront. You also have to ask people to confront you when you need it.

Confrontation is an extension of love. It's an extension of leadership. It's an extension of caring about the world around us and the people entrusted to us. Without it, we are just cowards in a declining universe.

The truth is that low-level confrontations keep the big confrontations from being necessary. It is like the difference between low-level explosions and the gigantic explosion of a bomb. Low-level explosions actually power us forward. Your car is powered by a series of rapid, low-level explosions. That plane you flew recently is powered by low-level explosions. These micro-explosions are a form of fuel, just like low-level confrontations. They move lives and organizations forward, ever refining, ever draining off toxic attitudes and behaviors before they reach flood stage. Avoid healthy small explosions and big ones will occur.

If I love my wife, I will confront—it sounds like a big deal but all I mean is "mention" or "challenge"— what I see that is destructive to her. It isn't picking at her. It isn't criticism. Well-intended confrontation is the fruit of loving her. I want her to be her best. I want her to be respected. I want her to never be ridiculed or embarrassed if I can help it.

So, "Baby, that blouse shows more than you want it to when you bend over." Or, "Honey, folks might not understand what you mean when you say that." Or, "I'm not concerned about it as your husband, honey, but I want you to think about how it might look to others."

There are weightier confrontations people must have, of course—about the sexual abuse or the theft or the affair. But the truth is that regular, low-level confrontations usually make the big ones—and the explosions they can lead to—unnecessary. We keep short accounts. We check in with each other. We take care of business before things go awry. This is what low-level confrontation does.

The wise leader builds a culture of redemptive confrontation around him or her. No one wants to hurt or embarrass, but everyone cares about each other enough to risk what must be risked to address the ticking time bomb. Or maybe just the small matter that might lead to embarrassment or no dates or lost sales or uninspired employees.

The sign to look for, then, is when a leader sidesteps the process of confrontation. Watch for this, particularly if the culture around that leader never included loving confrontation to begin with.

It means there is no line of defense. A leader can fall, and no one will ever step up to offer a challenge.

When a leader avoids, resists, or won't allow well-intended, friendly confrontation that is only meant to do him and his organization a great deal of good—then a crash is coming.

A culture of healthy confrontation is a culture of growth, trust, and achievement. A culture of cowardly avoidance is a culture of death to every area of life.

5. Losing Trusted Friendships

I'VE ALREADY MENTIONED THAT THE two most frequently named reasons for a crash are isolation and being out of season. It's true and we should watch for these trends diligently. Yet my consultant friends agree with me that the clearest indicator of a man's decline is the state of his friendships.

Friendships are hard, especially for men. They come naturally in high school and college, but as obligations grow in life, deep friendships with other men drop off. Time and again I have worked with a man in his fifties or sixties who simply cannot name a single close friend. He has acquaintances. He has golf buddies and lunch buddies and maybe even a guy in his neighborhood he can watch a game with from time to time. If I ask him if he has a best friend, though, he stares at me blankly. You can tell he's trying to figure out right there in front of me how he got himself into this friendless condition when his best buds used to mean so much to him.

I've often dreamed of teaching a course to young leaders in which I would bring together all of the factors of happiness and success as happy and successful people see them. I'm all for teaching the technicalities needed for life and profession. I'm also an advocate for teaching the "soft skills." By this I mean those intangibles that the wealthy and effective say are so important to them. In a course like this, the art of friendship would be among the leading topics.

Most people in the Western world today are living lives that are relationally a mile wide and an inch deep. They find themselves awash in a sea of casual relationships. Twitter and Facebook give them virtual friendships that offer only techno-chatter passing itself off as community. The result is that most leaders would die of neglect if they needed even one friend to show up at an inconvenient time to rescue them.

The wise build their lives differently. They not only understand the power and joy of friendship, they know they need it. They need a band of brothers or sisters who love them but aren't afraid of them. They need the fun, the rowdiness, and the companionship, but they also sense that they just need someone who knows them and won't let them go.

Let me give you a pet opinion of mine. In church cultures and recovery cultures, for example, there are things called "accountability groups." The idea is that you drive to a meeting, usually at some breakfast spot, and tell people how your life is going so they can pray for you or encourage you or hold you accountable about sobriety or gambling and the like.

Now, it sounds good, but it just won't work. You see, this is artificial community. It's artificial friendship. Let me tell you straight up that if we have to wait, first, until I figure out what is wrong with me and then, second, until I work up the courage to tell someone and then, third, until my accountability meeting comes around once a week or a month—I'm screwed! I'll be dead somewhere! I'm just not that smart, courageous, or patient.

No, what I need is a band of brothers who love me with their whole hearts but will risk our relationship in a heartbeat to keep me from harm—even from harming myself. I need people who are close enough to know what is wrong with me before I know it.

My guys hear the slip in my language before I know it is there. They see the extra glass of wine. They notice the third glance at the bosomy waitress and put it together with the impatient tone of my last phone call with my wife and they sense trouble. They land on me like a jaguar descending from a tree. They are smarter than I am, they are tougher, and they have no intention of letting me talk my way out of anything. They want to know—and they want to know now or they will pound me to death—what's going on at home or what that anger is all about or why I seem intent on eating myself into a coma. They also know that Oreos are my drug of choice, that I hide from my buddies when I'm hurt, and that when I get very, very quiet a storm is approaching.

They know these things because we have life together. And they are not afraid of me. They love me as I love them—as men who know how important friendships are in this lonely world but who will risk losing each other to help each other out.

I'm fortunate. Most men and most women don't have this. Men have almost no deep relationships at all when they reach midlife. Women often have a wide variety of friends who will meet them for coffee but, like the men, no one who is all in—completely committed to being there. I mean there at the emergency room at three in the morning. At the funeral. When there is nothing to do but stand there and cry. Or when there is nothing to do but raise a glass and dance the next song. They are there. It's a lifetime thing. And most people living in the Western world never know what it is like to be this kind of friend or to have this kind of friend.

For those who have friends—and most leaders are magnetic enough to have accumulated many friends through the years—the state of these friendships reflect the state of the leader. I've never worked on a crash or helped prevent one where the close friends weren't in some way registering what was happening in the soon-to-be-crashed leader's life.

Joe had been hurt and he was angry. His friends reported that Joe had been a jackass at their last get-together and then he had stormed out. Joe's friends might not have known what the cause was, but they knew Joe was hurt, angry, and heading for trouble. They knew to be on guard.

Sometimes friends know more than that. Old Tim was too happy. He was forcing it. *That fool is hiding something. That idiot is trying to keep something from us? From the guys who know him better than anybody and who don't deserve to be lied to? Okay, call Bob. We're going to do some butt-kicking at Tim's place tonight.*

When a leader is heading for trouble, he or she is either too present to their friends or too removed. The friends feel the anger, the duplicity, the "I-Give-Up" masquerading as "Let's-Party" and the "She's-Driving-Me-Nuts" that sounds like a cry for "Road Trip!!" when it actually wants "Uncomplicated-Girls-Behaving-Badly." Friends know. They are the mirror for a wise leader. They are the roving intervention. They are the cops on the road to disaster saying, "This road is closed. Turn around and go back."

Friends are a sign. So is the absence of friends. If a man is thirty and can't name a close friend, he's already dysfunctional. If he's forty and can't name a friend to watch a game with or whom he trusts to help his wife when he's out of town or whom he wants to just hang with absent any purpose at all but enjoying the moment, then he's a fool. If this is true at fifty, he's already in trouble—and dying.

Watch friendships. The trend of decline will be registered in them first. If they've been pushed away, there's trouble coming. If they can't get him to go home, something's wrong. If he's trying to get his posse to join him in some form of escape from real life, something is wrong. And if a man has no friends, something is terribly wrong with his soul and has been for quite a while.

6. Forgetting Fun

I WON'T TAKE LONG WITH THIS ONE. IT IS very important but I find that all I have to do is describe it, call for it, and turn the troops lose. The rest comes naturally.

You may be surprised when I say that one of the indicators of a nearing crash is when life as we are living it has no room for fun. Actually, I mean more than fun. I mean wildness, rowdiness, full-bodied abandonment, letting the soul roar through the body.

Sound like too much for you? All I'm really talking about is a sport, some excitement, some unrestrained living for just a little while.

Men and women both need it. We are all overly domesticated. We are too civilized every second of the day. We live from our heads and ask our bodies and our inner savage to behave. We're adults after all. We've no time for childish ways.

Now, don't worry. I'm not going to expound some airy theory from Sigmund Freud or try to dazzle you with pop psychobabble. It's really simple, actually. We are more than one thing. We have a spirit. We have a body. We have a mind. Things like emotions and the will are in there too, probably living somewhere in the borderland between the mind and the spirit. We are more than one thing.

But you wouldn't know it by how we live. We are ever starving most of who we are in deference to the mind we esteem beyond all else and all in order to live in an information age.

We end up living single-dimension lives. Beyond the need for exercise, we need the rowdy and the unrestrained. We need to get our "ya-ya's out." Thank you, Rolling Stones. We need to turn loose and not just at an annual vacation for a few days and not just once a decade when the old college gang gets together to drink a lot of beer.

Put a bunch of men in an empty break room and within minutes they are folding a piece of paper into a triangle and playing a table version of football. Ask a typical guy to throw away a can and he can't just do it normally. He becomes Michael Jordan and does a fade-away, double-pump, beyond-the-three-point-line jump shot like his life and the Bulls' championship depend on it. Ask him to watch his five-year-old son on a Saturday afternoon and it all ends in sweat, underwear, a torn-up house, and an imagined enemy who must be destroyed to save the world. Somehow the vacuum cleaner hose and a floor lamp play a role as well but no one but the two of them will ever know why.

Women are different, but not much. They need adventure of their own kind. It's usually relational adventure. That's why the Luscious Breath novels with Abs LongHair on the cover and a whole lot of dresses torn at the bosom somehow appeal to the ladies. Then there is dancing. And flirting. And shopping. And nearing the edge with the cocktail made with that peach liqueur. And that new dress that's a bit risqué. And walking the roaring surf at

Maui in the early morning with the Lover/Husband/
Man Toy knowing anything might happen.

We all need to press the boundaries. We all need
to push to the edge a bit. We bore even ourselves
to death if we don't. We get stale. And one day, if
we don't regularly let the pressure off, we'll find the
wildness we need in the adventure of an affair. Or,
as in one case I worked on, in stealing from grocery
stores even though we have millions in the bank.
Or the artificial adventure of fantasy and porn. Or
the manufactured adventure of becoming a Drama
Queen. Or even the oozy journey into the bottom
of a bottle of Jack Daniels. We will have our rowdy
adventures, even if they destroy our lives.

So we should have our planned distractions.
Men need to hit something, blow something up,
and bark at the moon. Women need not to feel bor-
ing and need to feel that their whole body is alive
and functioning. They need to feel that mystery
and possibilities still swirl about them. And they,
too, may need to blow something up or bark at
the moon.

Get a sport. Have a hobby. Get bruised and scraped doing something. Have a goal for how far you can run or how many pushups you can do or how badly Sarah is going down the next time we play tennis. Declare it. Write it on the wall. Tell your family you're going to do it and tell them to blow off when they laugh at you. Face a fear. Let your friends stand mouths gaping when you tell them you jumped out of an airplane or pet a shark or danced until breakfast and then experimented with adult smoothies until noon.

Now for the sign. If a leader has no outlet, no blow off, no place for risk and sore muscles and semi-safe recklessness, he's either heading for trouble or he lost parts of himself at the mall years ago. A woman can do exactly the same, except she becomes either the Wicked Witch of the West or some genderless creature for whom eating out is the big adventure.

Leadership presses us into single dimension lives. Press back. Do it in a healthy, constructive way or you'll do it in a way that blows up your life, but by the time you do you won't care anymore about the rubble.

Two quotes. Winston Churchill said, "We want engineers in the world but we don't want a world of engineers." In other words, we need more than the technical and the precise. And Eleanor Roosevelt said, "Do something every day that scares you." And then she either got in a biplane with a Tuskegee pilot or she became a delegate to the United Nations. Both scared her. Ah, but what a life she lived. Now *that* was a woman!

7. Perpetuating an Artificial Image

ONE OF THE GREAT JOYS OF MY LIFE IS the media training I do for high profile people. It is about the most thrilling work I know. Here's why.

Usually, by the time a person achieves prominence, they've had so much bad advice about how to speak in public that they have become unnatural and mechanical. This means they have also become ineffective. So my specialty is in helping public people find their authentic speaking voice and then strengthening that voice to serve the purpose of their lives. Little delights me as much as seeing a great leader find his or her voice and then use it to change lives for the better.

When we first start working with most leaders, though, it is torturous. Why? They are in the service of bad ideas. They have had too much bad advice, too much vanity disguised as wisdom planted in their minds. Usually, they've been coached to emulate someone they admire rather than just be themselves. They've tried to fulfill a vision of themselves that isn't genuine. It's difficult to watch because it makes them ineffective. They spend their energy trying to be what they can never be: someone else.

This dynamic reminds me of a scene in the movie *Seabiscuit* in which the horse's trainer tells the jockey to just let Seabiscuit run wide open awhile. When he does, the regal animal not only looks magnificent—he had been wobbly and uncontrollable before—but he also runs at amazing speeds. The trainer explains, "Sometimes they are so beat up, they've forgotten what it's like to be a horse."

That's what I find with many of our media training clients. They've forgotten what it is to be themselves. Once they rediscover themselves and harness their strengths to the principles of good communication, it is astonishing how powerful they become.

The short lesson is that to serve an artificial image of yourself is to become a weaker version of yourself.

This is why one of the signs of an impending leadership crash is when a leader tethers himself to exaggerated branding. It means he makes promises he can't keep. It is exhausting. It is dishonest. It keeps him in constant turmoil since his performance is more of an act than a matter of leading in an authentic way. The crush between the real man and the artificial brand is often too much. A crash results.

I remember reading something that the fallen television preacher Jim Bakker once wrote. He said, "My dream became bigger and bigger. And the box got bigger—the outside, the buildings. And soon the box got bigger than the message, than the truth. I had to raise about $1 million every two days just to stay alive. And the image destroyed the reality."

The image destroyed the reality. I've seen it hundreds of times. A hotshot leader has a reputation as a giant killer when he isn't. He's just good at spin. The family-run church becomes a monster that must be served. The family hardly has time to deal with real matters in a genuine way. Instead they spend all their time and conversation devising strategies to prop up "the ministry"—which they speak of like it is in the room with them—at all costs. The weight of it all is killing them. A manager is known as a sales magnet, but he's taking credit for another man's statistics and he knows it. The pressure between what is true and what others perceive to be true is nearly destroying his life.

In scenarios like these, the crash usually comes not because the leader can't sustain the image, but because he doesn't want to anymore. He engineers his own crash, like a man setting fire to a house that feels like a prison to him. Everyone else bemoans the loss of the house. The man/arsonist feels free. No price was too high to pay for getting out of that prison. This is what many leaders feel: they are prisoners of their own branding, their own spin.

Remember, meaningful branding grows from a combination of vision, values, and reality. Vain branding leads to a tyranny of the brand—which almost always leads to a leadership crash.

8. Serving the Schedule

—————

IN 2005, I HAD THE PRIVILEGE OF BEING imbedded with our troops in Iraq. While I was there, I learned a huge amount about Post-Traumatic Stress Disorder (PTSD). What I learned caused me to agonize for our troops, and then it helped me to gain some important perspective on how leaders function.

It turns out that PTSD is, in part, a result of not having answers to some important questions. One of those questions is "Why do I do what I do?"

This question isn't necessarily about the calling and identity of the individual soldier. It is about every soldier having a moral rationale for the things he or she must do in war. In the military, duty reigns. You rise early. You rush from obligation to obligation, assignment to assignment. You fulfill a set of orders and wait for yet another set. In war, these orders often involve danger and death. You fall exhausted into troubled sleep at night only to rise early the next morning and do it all again.

Here is what an army psychologist told me: "Soldiers don't mind doing what they have to do. Post-Traumatic Stress Disorder occurs when they can no longer connect to why they do it."

One of the great casualties of war is connection to the reasons for fighting the war. This means that a soldier's lot becomes duty without meaning, duty without purpose, duty without the framing that provides a moral mandate for his fight. Given that he must sometimes kill and destroy, it is all the more important that he keeps at the forefront of his mind some sense of moral purpose, what a few Marines described to me as "a righteous mandate for our part of the war."

Otherwise, schedule rules without vision. Duty reigns with no meaningful purpose. The hours issue demands but draw the warrior no closer to his aim because he has no aim. Duty reigns for its own sake.

Now, the lot of a leader in a manufacturing plant in St. Louis is certainly not as treacherous as the lot of a soldier at war, but lessons from the experience of the one do translate to the experience of the other.

All leaders are busy. They rush from meeting to meeting, trip to trip, and they are expected to care intently about each minute, each word, each decision. Unless there is some process for keeping the schedule and the purpose aligned, disorders of every kind set in. And a leadership crash is not far off.

The disconnect between schedule and vision occurs more easily for high-level leaders because they put their scheduling in the hands of others. They "have a two o'clock with Johnson in shipping" and "lunch at Morton's with the finance committee of the board" and it is all sandwiched between a dozen other meetings in the day. Sometimes, no one seems to remember why all this was scheduled, and when that happens, just getting through it becomes the goal. This is when burnout and lost productivity and the search for an escape hatch begin.

Once the schedule ceases being a method to sanely achieve predetermined ends, the leader has stepped on a conveyor belt—or a roller coaster—over which he feels he has no control. The schedule becomes an animal we ride each day hoping not to fall off and be trampled. It is not a tool. It is not the planned fine-tuning of a vision. It is not the product of goals. It is a cruel master.

This attitude toward the schedule leads to every kind of crash. Leaders drink because they want to relax and forget. They are pulled away from family and even themselves. They don't have time to sharpen the saw, refocus the vision, and do the work with wise pacing and strategic intent. They work out too little, eat too much, discuss rather than lead, put themselves at the behest of all who ask for time, and leave off fine-tuning the battle plan with the generals in order to appease every fresh-faced captain in the field.

And they grow to resent it. Resentment nearly always leads to entitlement: "I deserve that drink. I deserve that dessert. I deserve time with the shapely young lady at the bar. I deserve to divert some of that money into my account. I deserve more respect and I'll get it where I can. I deserve more than I'm getting at home given how hard I work. I deserve…."

Here is the lesson: A schedule-driven leader has already given up the lead. Stop. Take stock. Cancel everything for a few days, remember who you are and what you are about. Perhaps bring in a few trusted advisors to help you fine tune. Then, refashion the schedule-making machinery into a purring sports car rather than an old clunker crammed with backseat drivers.

A leadership crash often occurs when a leader is ground under by schedule. Tame the schedule by reclaiming the reason for having a schedule in the first place: strategically achieving goals.

9. Building a Third World

———

WE THINK OF THE WORDS "THIRD world" in terms of the less developed nations on earth, but I want to use them to describe a realm that dysfunctional leaders create for themselves. To do this, I'm going to have to beat up a bit on President William Jefferson Clinton.

It is unfortunate that Mr. Clinton has become a symbol of so much that goes wrong with leadership. He is a gifted man whose presidency left us some good things. Surely we can agree upon this, whatever our politics. Still, he behaved in such a way that he made himself the archetype of adolescent behavior in high office. We should learn from his mistakes. Even he has said that he hopes other leaders will avoid his follies. Let's do.

When Mr. Clinton was president, he apparently allowed the stress of office to do two things that no leader can afford. His duties both bored him and drained the affection he had once shared with his wife. These are two dynamics that never lead to good things.

Faced with inner emptiness when at work and at home, Clinton started scanning for some other form of excitement. Remember what I said earlier: Some men pursue affairs merely for the adventure. Starved for excitement and bored by their lives, they create—and this is overstating to make a point—a game, a miniature world in which intrigue and pursuit and, yes, sex and romance, distract from soul-numbing routine. This is apparently what Mr. Clinton did with Monica Lewinsky.

We don't need to get into the details of that troubling episode in our nation's history. There is one part of the Clinton/Lewinsky affair, though, that will help us avoid our own leadership crashes.

I'll let the *Los Angeles Times* state the critical fact: "White House logs reveal that Hillary Clinton was in the West Wing during the same hours that Bill Clinton was with Monica Lewinsky in the president's private office." You see, Mr. Clinton found himself caught between the drudgery of his work in the Oval Office and the chill of his life at home. What did he do? He created that Third World I mentioned. He met with a twenty-something intern in his private office and started enjoying what he didn't have in the two places that defined his life—office and home. He created a Third World in order to have what he wanted but was not getting from his life as it was.

This is one of the most common patterns of unfulfilled leaders. They create Third Worlds. They usually have enough money to pay for it and enough mobility to allow for it and enough skill at lying to hide it. So, when leading and life at home prove unfulfilling, they find an apartment somewhere. Or the hotel just off of Whitehall in London. Or the suite at the friend's house in Cuernavaca, Mexico. And they stock their Third World with whatever they've been starving for given the meager offerings in the rest of their lives.

The Third World isn't just about the adventure of an affair, though. It can be about the club membership. I've known executives of both genders to ruin their lives gambling and drinking on private planes. Another created his toxic Third World by building out a basement—in the bottom of his company's skyscraper! For a porn theater! There was also the CEO who built a hunting cabin just to be alone for a change. It was his version of the Third World. He spent more and more time there. And then he killed himself with his hunting rifle. His suicide note said he was too lonely to live on.

Of course, there is nothing wrong with apartments in London or private planes or hunting cabins. Nor was there anything wrong with an intern being in Mr. Clinton's private office. It is what the unfulfilled soul of the leader makes of the location, of that halfway world between work and home, that makes the Third World such a legend of leadership destruction.

This Third World is easy to find once you know what to look for. It is the place of artificial fulfillment the leader creates as a haven from responsibility, as a storehouse for answers to his unmet needs. For the discerning, it has the vague appearance of a very stylish tomb, because it is where great leaders go to bury their careers in the soil of self-pity and entitlement.

10. Losing the Poetry

―――――

THE FINAL OF OUR TEN SIGNS OF A leadership crash is really the early warning sign of all the rest. It can be a sign of its own, but it more usually anticipates—even creates—all the other conditions that indicate an oncoming crash. It is simply this: losing the poetry of what you do.

There is a movie that illustrates this beautifully. It is the 1987 film *Broadcast News* starring Holly Hunter, William Hurt, and Albert Brooks. The film opens with Hunter, who plays a television news producer, waking up in the morning, sitting at the side of her bed, and moving herself to tears. Then, satisfied, she goes on with her day. We don't know why. Only later does she explain. She's told herself that when the tragedies she has to deal with in her job no longer move her to tears, she'll stop. She'll know she's become numb and that she needs to leave, to find some other work where she can keep her heart engaged.

It is a perfect lesson for leaders. We usually do what we do because we were first moved by it. In ministry, in the military, in building, in leading teams—in whatever we did when we began—we found something about it that was beautiful. There was a poetry to it. Call it love.

And let's not make this too high and holy. A man can have a successful career because he loves people and finds beauty in spreadsheets. A man can love how bricks look in a well-crafted wall or how well-done sutures leave only a slight scar or how his staff members dance with their spouses at the New Year's party when they feel secure about their future and valued as part of an effective team. This is the poetry, the reasons beyond the practical reasons for what we do.

It is an art of leadership to keep the higher reasons for what we do before our own eyes and before the eyes of those who serve with us. It is the Great

Alignment. It is the homing device of destiny. It is the GPS of happiness and greatness and true prosperity. Lose this signal, and all goes wrong.

This is the heart of motivation. It is the basis of possessing a winning manner. It is what produces the magnetism that leaders need. Much of our leadership theory today speaks of fine-tuning the characteristics of the leader. There is some benefit in this. Great leadership, though, is great because it is committed to a great cause, purpose, or ideal.

There is no natural reason that Winston Churchill should have been the greatest leader of his generation. He was great because he was committed to the great cause of Britain and Western civilization. There is no natural reason that Steve Jobs should have been so successful. If you read his story, you'll find that he was committed not just to the technology but the poetry of the technology. So it goes with most great leaders.

I've heard hotel maids tell their fellow workers that they tried to do every part of their job well for God, for their children's future, and to impress the boss with what people of their race and color could do. That's the poetry. I've had a taxi driver tell me he wanted each of his passengers to have their best taxi experience in his cab. Why? Because he was a Kurdish immigrant who was tearfully grateful to America. He wanted to honor the gift of his citizenship. I've had an Ivy League MBA tell me that he realized he had a gift for generating wealth and he wanted to use that gift to lift the poor families of Appalachia. He had seen a documentary about Robert Kennedy going into the Appalachian Mountains and witnessing horrific poverty. As a young man, this MBA had traveled there himself. The poverty was bad, he said, but not so entrenched that it couldn't be fixed in a generation. He wanted it to be his generation.

This may not be your poetry, the beauty that calls to you in your profession. Frankly, it isn't mine. But your version of this poetry exists, either for the work you do or the work you are hoping to do. Find it. Keep it. Write it on a wall. Declare it aloud. Make it the measure of what you hope to achieve.

But hear this: Every leadership crash I've ever seen came after the leader got so numb he couldn't find the poetry with a flashlight. It was then one of the other dynamics I've described in this little book kicked in. The brilliant lady who rescued the leading tech firm got out of season and crashed. Why? It all became procedures and processes for her and she lost sight of the beauty. The congressman got bitter, forgot who he served and why, forgot his immigrant father's tears when he put a US flag in his yard or when he had the privilege of voting. He got hardened, got dry, got myopic and small and died—in the appropriations scandal he was glad his father was not alive to see.

Tiger forgot the privilege of playing the game. Nixon forgot to fashion a future rather than avenge a past. Sandusky forgot the sacred trust of coaching and the glory of young boys becoming men.

In truth, what I'm describing is a form of gratitude for what we get to do. If we can get up in the morning and say, "Look what I get to do" and say it with excitement, gratitude, and joy, we're safe. I get to lead these people. I get to guide a great company. I get to steer the direction of my city. I get to produce wealth and fashion young executives along the way. I get to teach. I get to write. I could be digging ditches. I could be gutting fish. I'm going to go to the 54th floor and write a check to put inner city kids in elite colleges because I get to work for that kind of company.

Gratitude for the beauty. And for a life inspired by beauty. And for the love of the game, whatever the game is. And for the poetry that makes it all about more than mere duty.

There is no part of leadership not ennobled by keeping this thing I call the poetry at heart. And every part of leadership is made poorer by its absence. More to the point of our theme here, leadership crashes start in the hearts of leaders unprotected by gratitude and love and the call of the poetry.

Don't pass this one by because it is a bit ethereal and perhaps artsy and emphasizes feeling over fact. It is the core battle of leadership. In fact, leadership doesn't happen without it. Not the real thing. Management, maybe. Command perhaps. But not leadership.

The sign? When was the last time that inner joy—if not your version of Holly Hunter's tears—filled your heart at the thought of what you get to do? Keep it if you have it. Find it if you've lost it. Know that the crash is waiting if you don't.

Conclusion

Now, take a moment and look over this list.

1. **Being Out of Season**
2. **Choosing Isolation**
3. **Defining Episodes of Bitterness**
4. **Evading Confrontation**
5. **Losing Trusted Friendships**
6. **Forgetting Fun**
7. **Perpetuating an Artificial Image**
8. **Serving the Schedule**
9. **Building a Third World**
10. **Losing the Poetry**

These are not just academic topics. They are not terms for describing your friends. This is a checklist. For you. These are signs of looming disaster. Do they point to any realities in your life? Are they warning you of something you already know to be real about who you are and how you lead? If so, you already know what to do. You might need help. It might take some time. But you are gifted enough to achieve the turnaround you need.

Finally, remember this lesson from that great Disney movie *The Lion King*. At one point in this brilliant cartoon and stage play, the ghost of the great lion Mufasa appears to his son and says, "Remember who you are!"

That's it! *Remember who you are.* Before the crash. Before unproductive years. Before the addiction and the humiliation and the broken lives. *Remember who you are.* It is the cure. Forgetting leads to the crash, the end of aimless souls and spoiled children with money enough for their own destruction. Remembering, though, is how we restore the art of effective leadership and fulfilled lives.

CONNECT WITH
**STEPHEN
MANSFIELD**

STEPHEN MANSFIELD.TV

 @MansfieldWrites

 MansfieldWrites

 MansfieldWrites

 MansfieldWrites